WELCOME TO MY COUNTRY

Welcome to
POLAND

Gareth Stevens Publishing
A WORLD ALMANAC EDUCATION GROUP COMPANY

Written by
UMAIMA MULLA-FEROZE/PAUL GRAJNERT

Edited in USA by
DOROTHY L. GIBBS

Designed by
GEOSLYN LIM

Picture research by
SUSAN JANE MANUEL

First published in North America in 2003 by
Gareth Stevens Publishing
A World Almanac Education Group Company
330 West Olive Street, Suite 100
Milwaukee, Wisconsin 53212 USA

Please visit our web site at:
www.garethstevens.com
For a free color catalog describing
Gareth Stevens' list of high-quality
books and multimedia programs,
call 1-800-542-2595 (USA) or
1-800-387-3178 (CANADA).
Gareth Stevens Publishing's fax: (414) 332-3567.

© **TIMES MEDIA PRIVATE LIMITED 2003**
Originated and designed by
Times Editions
An imprint of Times Media Private Limited
A member of the Times Publishing Group
Times Centre, 1 New Industrial Road
Singapore 536196
http://www.timesone.com.sg/te

Library of Congress Cataloging-in-Publication Data
Mulla-Feroze, Umaima.
Welcome to Poland / Umaima Mulla-Feroze and Paul Grajnert.
p. cm. — (Welcome to my country)
Includes bibliographical references and index.
Summary: An introduction to the geography, history, government,
economy, people, and culture of Poland.
ISBN 0-8368-2545-4 (lib. bdg.)
1. Poland—Juvenile literature. [1. Poland.]
I. Grajnert, Paul. II. Title. III. Series.
DK4147.M85   2003
943.8—dc21   2002030282

Printed in Malaysia

1 2 3 4 5 6 7 8 9 07 06 05 04 03

PICTURE CREDITS
Allsport/Stu Forster: 36
ANA Press Agency: 7 (top), 27 (top)
Art Directors and Trip Photo Library: 17,
    19, 22, 25, 45
Camera Press Ltd.: 7 (bottom), 8 (bottom),
    16 (both), 18, 24, 26 (bottom),
    28 (bottom), 33, 34 (both), 40 (top)
Sue Cunningham Photographic:
    1, 41 (bottom)
Embassy of the Republic of Poland: 44
Focus Team – Italy: 3 (center), 3 (bottom),
    21 (both), 23 (bottom), 30 (both), 31,
    35, 37, 40 (bottom), 43
Getty Images/HultonArchive: 10 (both),
    11 (both), 13 (bottom), 15 (top),
    29 (both)
Bridget Gubbins: 4, 9 (both), 23 (top)
PAI Fotografia: 8 (top), 12, 13 (top),
    28 (top)
Chip & Rosa Maria Petersen: 2, 32 (top), 39
Reuters/HultonArchive: 15 (bottom)
Topham Picturepoint: cover, 14 (both),
    20 (bottom), 27 (bottom), 32 (bottom),
    38, 41 (top)
Travel Ink: 3 (top), 5, 6, 20 (top), 26 (top)

Digital Scanning by Superskill Graphics Pte Ltd

Contents

Words that appear in the glossary are printed in **boldface** type the first time they occur in the text.

Welcome to Poland!

The Republic of Poland is one of the most populated countries in Central Europe. Ruled by **communists** from 1945 to 1989, Poland today has a **democratic** government, with rapid social and economic growth. Let's learn about Poland and its people.

The Flag of Poland

Poland's national flag, which was officially adopted in 1919, is white on top and red on the bottom. White represents peace. Red symbolizes the blood of Polish **patriots** who died in their nation's struggle for peace.

The Land

With an area of 120,728 square miles (312,685 square kilometers), Poland is slightly smaller than the U.S. state of New Mexico. It is surrounded by the Baltic Sea and the countries of Russia and Lithuania to the north, Belarus and Ukraine to the east, Slovakia and the Czech Republic to the south, and Germany to the west. Warsaw is the largest city and the country's capital.

Below:
The southern town of Zakopane lies at the foot of the High Tatra Mountains, the highest range in the Carpathian Mountains.

Left: Poland has 2,369 miles (3,812 kilometers) of **navigable** rivers and canals and more than nine thousand lakes. Most of the lakes are located in the northeastern and western regions.

Most of Poland is flat. Its northern and central regions form a vast, fertile plain. Mountains in the south and the southwest belong to the Carpathian range or the Sudeten range. Mount Rysy, Poland's highest peak, is in the Carpathian's High Tatra Mountains.

Two important **waterways** crossing Poland's central plain are the Vistula, or Wisla, River and the Oder, or Odra, River. Both rivers flow north to the Baltic Sea, and both provide water and transportation routes for large cities.

Below: Pollution is a big problem in Poland's many rivers and lakes.

Climate

Poland's **moderate** climate has six seasons. Early spring weather, from March to May, varies from wintry to springlike. Late spring, in May and June, is sunny. A warm, rainy summer, with an average temperature of about 72° Fahrenheit (22° Celsius), starts in July. Autumn is warm in September, then turns cool and damp in October. December brings a snowy winter.

Above: Skiing is a popular winter activity in Poland.

Below: Southern Poland has a lot of snow in winter.

Plants and Animals

Forests of beech, fir, spruce, and pine in the southern mountains, along with the wetlands of the northeast, are the only major areas of Poland that remain undisturbed by human inhabitants.

Wolves and brown bears live in the mountain areas. Elk, deer, and wild sheep roam freely in the northeastern region. Birds found in Poland include Pomeranian eagles, tawny owls, and black storks. Salmon, trout, and carp are some of the fish in Poland's rivers.

Above: Bialowieza National Park, near Bialystok, has a large herd of rare European bison.

Below: This woman is using special equipment to track wolves in eastern Poland.

History

From about A.D.100, a group of Slavs known as the Polanie settled on the central plains of Poland. They later united with other Slavs to form the kingdom of Poland. King Mieszko I, of the Piast **dynasty**, who reigned from about 963 to 992, is considered the founder of the Polish state. Under the Piast dynasty (966–1382), Poland grew to be a major European power.

Below:
Mieszko I (*left*) and Wladyslaw II Jagiello (*right*), of the Jagiellon dynasty, were important Polish kings during the Middle Ages.

Left: Alexander I was elected king of Poland in 1501 and ruled until his death in 1506. This illustration of Alexander's coronation is from an ancient manuscript.

Kazimierz III (r. 1333–1370) was another famous Piast king. He made laws, developed trade, and allowed **persecuted** Jews to settle in Poland.

In 1386, Piast queen Jadwiga married the grand duke of Lithuania, Wladyslaw II Jagiello. Over two centuries, Jagiellon kings continued to increase Polish land. When that dynasty ended, the Sejm (SAY-um), a group of powerful nobles, elected Poland's kings until 1795.

Below: Poland's Queen Jadwiga believed strongly in education. She even donated her jewelry in order to reestablish the University of Kraków, renamed the Jagiellonian University after her death.

11

The Fall and Rise of Poland

Weak leadership, corruption, and constant fighting within the country led neighboring Russia, Prussia, and Austria to **annex** Poland's land. In 1772, Poland lost one-fourth of its territory to these countries.

Believing that political **reform** was the only way to free their country from foreign rule, the Sejm passed the Constitution of May 3. Russia, Prussia, and Austria saw this constitution as a threat. In 1793, Russian and Prussian

Left: *Battle at Grunwald* is an eighteenth-century painting showing Polish soldiers attacking German warriors in 1410.

Left: Invading Poland in 1939, Nazi troops set up road blocks.

troops invaded Poland and took more of its land. The Polish fought against these forces but were defeated in 1795.

With help from Britain, France, and the United States, Poland regained its independence, but not until after World War I (1914–1918). For the unstable Polish nation, however, independence was short-lived. World War II (1939–1945) started when Nazi Germany and the Soviet Union invaded Poland and took control of the country. After the war, Poland remained under Soviet communist rule for forty-four years.

Below: During World War II, the Nazis put to death millions of Polish Jews at **concentration camps** such as Auschwitz.

The Solidarity Movement

In 1980, factory workers throughout Poland went on strike, demanding democracy and more human rights. This Solidarity Movement, led by an electrician named Lech Walesa (1943–), succeeded. In 1989, in the nation's first open elections, Poles voted for noncommunist government.

Below (*left*): This street in Warsaw is an example of the destruction that occurred during World War II.

Below (*right*): The same street in 1955 shows how Warsaw was rebuilt after the war.

Maria Konopnicka (1842–1910)

Throughout her life, Polish poet and novelist Maria Konopnicka played an active role in organizations that protested the persecution of Poles by the Russians and the Prussians.

Tadeusz Mazowiecki (1927–)

Tadeusz Mazowiecki

An important anticommunist figure in the 1980s, lawyer and journalist Tadeusz Mazowiecki was elected Poland's first noncommunist leader after the war. As editor of the official publication of the Solidarnosc trade union, Mazowiecki played a major role in the Solidarity Movement.

Adam Malysz

Adam Malysz (1978–)

One of the world's top ski-jumpers, Adam Malysz has made this sport popular both in Poland and abroad. At the 2001 World Cup competition in Oslo, Norway, Malysz jumped a near-record 408 feet (124 meters).

Government and the Economy

Poland is a **constitutional republic**. In 1997, the country adopted a new constitution that guarantees the rights of the Polish people and sets up a national government. The president, who is elected by the people, and the prime minister, appointed by the president, lead the government. Laws are passed by a parliament with two chambers, the Senate and the Sejm.

Above: A special gallery in Poland's parliament allows members of the general public to view proceedings.

16

Parliament's 100 senators and the 460 deputies of the Sejm, or House of Representatives, are elected by the people, all for four-year terms. In Poland's justice system, the president appoints Supreme Court judges, and the Sejm selects the judges who serve on the Constitutional Tribunal.

Poland has three different levels of local government: village or small town, county, and provincial.

The Economy

When communism ended in Poland, the country's economy changed from state-controlled to a free market. More than 70 percent of all Polish goods and services today are provided by private companies. About 25 percent of the total workforce have agricultural jobs. Another 25 percent are employed in the manufacturing, construction, and mining industries. The rest work in service jobs, such as transportation.

Above: Among the countries in Eastern Europe, Poland has one of the strongest economies, and new laws have made setting up businesses easier.

Natural Resources

Poland's fertile agricultural land is its main natural resource. Almost half of the land is **cultivated**. Crops include potatoes, fruits, and leafy vegetables. Forests, which cover almost 30 percent of the country, are valuable resources for Poland's important timber and paper industries. Poland also has rich coal and metal deposits for mining and is a world leader in silver production.

Below: Many old factories that were built when Poland was a communist country are now worthless and are being torn down.

People and Lifestyle

About 97 percent of Poland's more than 38 million people are Polish. Among the remaining 3 percent are Germans, Ukrainians, Lithuanians, Slovaks, Belorussians, and Romany Gypsies. Before World War II, over three million Jews lived in Poland, but after their brutal treatment by the Nazis, only a small group remains.

Above: Romany Gypsies are one of several **ethnic** minorities living in Poland. The largest **minority group** is German.

Left: Weddings in Poland can be as simple as getting a license from a government office or as elaborate as an all-night party with live music and plenty of food. These newlyweds were married in traditional clothing.

Under Poland's constitution, all citizens have equal rights, so minority groups can keep their own cultures and teach their native languages to their children. Some minorities even have representatives in the Sejm.

Opposite: Polish families, especially those with young children, spend a lot of time together.

Below: This family from the southern city of Zakopane is sharing a meal. In Poland, most leisure activities also involve the whole family.

Family Life

Polish families are close-knit. Parents and grandparents often live with their children and grandchildren. As adults, most Poles do not move very far from the places where they were born.

Women in Poland

In communist Poland, women were considered equal to men and were represented in Parliament, although few had active roles in politics. In democratic Poland, the traditional women's roles of homemakers and mothers are changing, and Polish women have set up organizations that discuss women's issues.

Above: Dressed in colorful ethnic clothing for a local festival in Wroclaw, these women look very traditional, but since the fall of communism in 1989, women's roles in Poland have changed.

City and Rural Life

Poles are typically gracious and well mannered, addressing strangers as *pan* (pan), or "sir," and *pani* (pan-EE), or "madam." The lifestyle of city dwellers is very different from Poles living in rural areas. People in Poland's modern cities are generally better educated and have more money. Most people living in rural Poland are poor, less educated, and old-fashioned in their ways. They do not trust the changes that have been taking place in Polish society.

Above: In some of Poland's rural areas, people still live in cottages with **thatch** roofs.

Below: Although most Polish farms today have modern machinery, some farmers still use horses to plow the fields.

Education

Every child in Poland between the ages of seven and seventeen must go to school. The Ministry of National Education runs most of the country's schools. A few are privately owned.

After six years of primary, or elementary, school, students must pass an examination to enter junior high school. Another examination, taken after three years of junior high,

Below:
Some of Poland's elementary schools and high schools are run by the Catholic Church.

Above:
A performance
by a student
choir is part of
the ceremony for
this university
graduation.

qualifies students for three years of high school. Those who earn a high school certificate can then enroll at a university. Students who do not go to high school can prepare to enter the workforce by attending a **vocational** school for two or three years.

Poland has many technical colleges and universities. Founded in 1364, the Jagiellonian University of Kraków is one of the oldest universities in Europe.

Religion

Roman Catholicism is Poland's main religion. This religion has an important place in the country's history because Poland was first recognized as a nation when its leaders became Catholics in A.D. 966. Approximately 95 percent of Poles are Roman Catholics. The rest belong to Eastern Orthodox, Protestant, or other faiths. For many modern Poles, however, practicing their religion has become less important than in the past.

Polish Jews

Although Poland has always claimed to have a policy of **religious tolerance**, Polish Jews were often forced to live in **ghettos**, away from the Catholics. During World War II, Polish Catholics showed little concern for the thousands of Jews being killed by the Nazis. In Jedwabne, Catholic Poles even killed their Jewish neighbors. Approximately 10,000 Jews still live in Poland today.

Above: Only about 75 percent of the Catholics in Poland practice their faith.

Below: Orthodox Christians attend a church service in Kraków.

Language

Almost all people in Poland speak Polish, the country's official language. The Polish language belongs to the western Slavic language group and uses the Roman, or Latin, alphabet.

The Polish alphabet has thirty-two letters. Special accent marks on some letters determine how they sound. The sound of *ó*, for example, is "OOH." Putting certain letters together creates other sounds, such as *sz* for "SH."

Above: Many old Polish manuscripts and books can be found outside of Poland, some at the Library of Congress in Washington, D.C.

Left: These posters are promoting the election of Tadeusz Mazowiecki, who was Poland's first noncommunist prime minister.

Literature

Pan Tadeusz, a poem written by Adam Mickiewicz in 1834, is one of Poland's most famous literary works. Its story reflects the hope for Poland's liberation during the Napoleonic wars. The well-known novel *Quo Vadis?* was written by Henryk Sienkiewicz, who won the Nobel Prize for Literature in 1905. In 1996, Wislawa Szymborska became the first Polish woman, and only the ninth woman ever, to earn this award.

Above:
Joseph Conrad (*left*), author of *Lord Jim* (1900) and *Heart of Darkness* (1902), was Polish, but he always wrote in English. Because of strict communist controls on what writers could say and not say, Jerzy Kosinski (*right*) and other Polish authors chose to leave the country and write in **exile**.

Arts

Folk art has been popular in Poland for a long time. It is an interesting hobby as well as a means of preserving Polish history. *Wycinanki* (vee-chee-NAN-kee) is a form of folk art in which dyed paper is cut or torn into designs. For the most elaborate designs, layers of paper are glued together. Weaving is an ancient folk art. Traditional materials such as flax and wool are used to make clothing, blankets, and other everyday items.

Above: Carving decorative wooden plates and statues is one of many forms of folk art in Poland.

Left: Wood sculptures like these, which were made in Zakopane, are often on display in Polish homes.

Making **Nativity** scenes, or *szopka* (SHOP-kah), out of paper, cardboard, beads, sequins, and colored foil is a Christmas tradition in Kraków.

Folk Dancing

Folk dancing in Poland brings people together and keeps traditions alive. Polish folk dances include the *mazur* (mah-ZOOR) and the *kujawiak* (koo-yah-wee-AHCK).

Polish Classical Music

Frédéric Chopin was Poland's most famous classical music **composer**. He used Polish folk melodies in his works and is known especially for his more than two hundred pieces of piano music.

Stanislaw Moniuszko and Henryk Wieniawski are also well-known Polish composers of the nineteenth century. Modern composers include Henryk Gorecki and Krzysztof Penderecki.

Jazz and Popular Music

After World War II, American jazz became very popular in Poland, even though it was banned by the country's communist government. Polish jazz musicians include Michal Urbaniak, a jazz violinist and composer, and Adam Makowicz, a jazz pianist.

Polish musicians play many styles of music that are popular in the United States and Western Europe, including rap, hip-hop, rock 'n' roll, and country.

Below: Along with American music and movies, Poland's young people seem to like American clothing. This young Pole is looking at a T-shirt that has a picture of famous American actress Marilyn Monroe on it.

Leisure

Summer is vacation time in Poland. Although some younger Poles like to travel around Europe and to other parts of the world, most Polish people stay within their own country. Beach resorts on the Baltic coast are popular vacation spots, and the Mazury Lakes region attracts campers and fishing enthusiasts. Rides along the canals that connect the many lakes offer spectacular views.

Above: In Gdansk, tourists can ride a barge down a canal.

Below: Poles flock to beaches on the Baltic coast to swim and sunbathe.

Polish families spend most of their leisure time together. Favorite outdoor activities include camping, sailing, and windsurfing. Popular weekend activities include mushroom picking in country forests and picnicking in city parks.

Some city dwellers own small plots of land in the country where they grow vegetable gardens. Many owners build a shack on the plot so they can spend the night when they visit their land.

Above: The High Tatra Mountains offer hikers many beautiful, scenic views. Hiking in the mountains of southern Poland is a favorite summer activity. In winter, Poles visit mountain resorts for skiing and snowboarding.

Left: During a soccer match in 2001, Wales player Ryan Giggs (*right*) kicks the ball past Poland's Tomasz Zdebel (*left*).

Sports

Soccer is Poland's most popular sport. While Poles of all ages enjoy it, young Poles will play anywhere they can find room enough to make a soccer field. The most devoted soccer fans, called *kibic* (kee-BEETS), are interested only in soccer news, scores, and players.

Poland has been a member of the Fédération Internationale de Football Association (FIFA) since 1923, and organized soccer in Poland dates back to 1919. Today, the country has four levels of professional teams. The First League, or highest level, has sixteen teams. First League players represent Poland in World Cup competition.

Basketball is another popular team sport in Poland. The country's top league has fifteen teams. Polish fans will even watch National Basketball Association (NBA) games from the United States on cable television.

Below: Chess is a favorite pastime for many Poles, and bridge is a popular card game.

Festivals

Many holidays in Poland are religious festivals, and Christmas Eve, or *Wigilia* (vee-GEE-lee-ah), is probably the most important one. Families enjoy a special meal together and exchange gifts. Then they attend a midnight mass called *Pasterka* (pas-TER-kah), or Shepherd's Mass, in honor of the shepherds at the birth of Jesus Christ. In pre-Christian times, this day celebrated the end of the harvest and the beginning of winter.

Below: Every year on Good Friday, the people of Kalwaria Zebrzydowska reenact the journey of Jesus Christ to Calvary, where he was crucified.

Easter is another important religious holiday in Poland. Preparations begin six weeks ahead, on Ash Wednesday. Willow twigs are cut for Palm Sunday, and children decorate eggs. On Easter morning, families go to church, then return home for a feast. Before eating, they break blessed eggs and share good wishes. The next day is for fun. Young Poles celebrate by throwing buckets of water over each other.

Above:
The traditional clothing worn for Polish festivals is both elaborate and colorful.

Food

Poles typically eat three meals a day, breakfast, lunch, and dinner, as well as an evening snack. Dinner, or *obiad* (OH-bee-ad), is the most important meal. It is served between 3:00 p.m. and 6:00 p.m., when everyone is home from work or school. Dinner usually includes soup, a main dish of meat and vegetables, dessert, and tea or coffee.

Above: Poles enjoy over one hundred kinds of sausages.

Below: Fried cheese is a Polish **delicacy**.

Left: Meat roasted outdoors is popular at feasts in towns and villages in the Sudeten Mountains.

Traditional Foods

Poland is famous for pork products such as pork chops and *kielbasa* (keel-BAH-zah), or sausages. Other traditional Polish foods include rye breads, sauerkraut, and *pierogi* (PEE-er-OHG-ee), which are dumplings, usually filled with meat, cabbage, cheese, or mushrooms. *Bigos* (BEE-gus) is a thick stew of cabbage and spiced meats. Poles also enjoy soups. *Chlodnik* (huh-LAWD-neek), a cold cucumber soup, is a summer favorite.

Below: Cookies and other sweets are an important part of any Polish feast. *Nalesniki* (NAL-esh-NYEE-kee) is a traditional Polish pancake.

41

A	B	C	D

International Boundary

Province Boundary

■ Capital

● City

⬆ Monument

River

1

Baltic Sea

LITHUANIA

RUSSIA

2 Gdansk ●

● Zulawka Sztumska

3 *Mazury Lakes Region*

1

4

GERMANY

Oder

6

7

Vistula

Jedwabne ●
Bialystok ●

8

Bialowieza National Park

BELARUS

2

5

Oder

N

WARSAW ■

9

3

10

● Wroclaw

11

● Lódz

12

13

Vistula

Sudeten Mountains

14

15
Kraków ●

Auschwitz Concentration Camp

● Kalwaria Zebrzydowska

High Tatra Mountains

▲ *Mount Rysy (8,199 ft/2,499 m)*

Zakopane ●

16

Carpathian Mountains

UKRAINE

4

CZECH REPUBLIC

POLAND

SLOVAKIA

Provinces

1 Zachodniopomorskie

2 Pomorskie

3 Warminsko-Mazurskie

4 Podlaskie

5 Lubuskie

6 Wielkopolskie

7 Kujawsko-Pomorskie

8 Mazowieckie

9 Lubelskie

10 Dolnoslaskie

11 Opolskie

12 Lodzkie

13 Swietokrzyskie

14 Slaskie

15 Malopolskie

16 Podkarpackie

Above: Once the capital city of Poland, Kraków still attracts many tourists.

Auschwitz
    Concentration
    Camp C4

Baltic Sea A1–C1
Belarus D1–D3
Bialowieza National
    Park D2
Bialystok D2

Carpathian
    Mountains
    C4–D4
Czech Republic
    A3–B4

Gdansk B1
Germany A1–A3

High Tatra
    Mountains C4

Jedwabne D2

Kalwaria
    Zebrzydowska
    C4
Kraków C4

Lithuania C1–D1
Lódz C3

Mazury Lakes
    Region C1–C2
Mount Rysy C4

Oder River
    A2–B4

Russia C1–D1

Slovakia B4–D4
Sudeten Mountains
    A3–B4

Ukraine D3–D4

Vistula River
    B1–C4

Warsaw C2
Wroclaw B3

Zakopane C4
Zulawka Sztumska
    C1

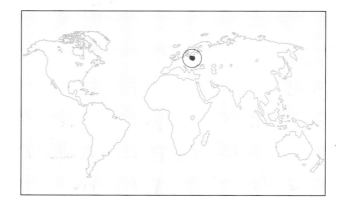

Quick Facts

Official Name   Republic of Poland

Capital   Warsaw

Official Language   Polish

Population   38,625,478 (2002 estimate)

Land Area   120,728 square miles (312,685 square km)

Highest Point   Mount Rysy 8,199 feet (2,499 m)

Border Countries   Belarus, Czech Republic, Germany, Lithuania, Russia, Slovakia, Ukraine

Mountain Ranges   Carpathian Mountains, Sudeten Mountains

Major Cities   Warsaw, Lódz, Kraków

Major Rivers   Vistula, Oder

Major Religions   Roman Catholicism, Eastern Orthodox, Protestantism

Important Holidays   Easter (March/April)

Constitution Day (May 3)

Independence Day (November 11)

Christmas Day (December 25)

Currency   Zloty (4.12 PLZ = U.S. $1 in 2002)

Opposite: Peanuts are one of Poland's many agricultural products.

Glossary

annex: take possession of a country or territory to increase the size or power of another country or territory.

communists: people that belong to a political system in which the government owns and controls all goods and resources.

composer: a person who writes music.

concentration camps: fenced, guarded areas where people are held prisoner, usually for political reasons.

constitutional republic: a nation or state that is governed by elected officials according to the principles of a written constitution.

cultivated: used for growing crops.

delicacy: an uncommon food that is considered a luxury.

democratic: related to a political system of self-rule through elected representatives.

dynasty: a family of rulers who inherit their power.

ethnic: related to a group of people from a particular country or culture.

exile: the state of being sent away by force from a person's homeland.

ghettos: poor areas of a city where many people of a particular minority group live because of economic or social pressures.

minority group: a small number of people within a much larger society, who share characteristics that are different from most other people's.

moderate: not too extreme in any way.

Nativity: the birth of Jesus Christ.

navigable: able to be traveled on, especially by ship or boat.

patriots: people who are extremely loyal to their countries or homelands.

persecuted: treated cruelly because of background, beliefs, or behaviors.

reform: change that is intended to correct faults or make improvements.

religious tolerance: allowing the practice of all faiths and religions.

thatch: plant materials such as straw, reeds, or palm leaves that are used as a covering to provide shelter.

vocational: related to an occupation, profession, or skilled trade.

waterways: bodies of water, such as rivers and canals, used for travel.

More Books to Read

Chopin. The World of Composers series. Greta Cencetti (McGraw-Hill)

Flowers on the Wall. Miriam Nerlove. (Margaret McElderry)

The Glass Mountain: Twenty-eight Ancient Polish Folktales and Fables. W. S. Kuniczak, editor (Hippocrene)

A Hero and the Holocaust: The Story of Janusz Korczak and His Children. David A. Adler (Holiday House)

Poland. Countries series. Kate A. Furlong (ABDO)

Poland. Countries of the World series. Suzanne Paul Dell'Oro (Bridgestone Books)

Poland. Festivals of the World series. Aldona Maria Zwierzynska-Coldicott (Gareth Stevens)

Poland. Postcards from series. Denise Allard (Raintree/Steck-Vaughn)

The Poles. We Came to North America series. Greg Nickles (Crabtree)

The Trumpeter of Krakow. Eric P. Kelly (Simon and Schuster)

Videos

Pope John Paul II. (Video Visions)

This Is Warsaw. (Polart)

Video Visits: Poland. (Questar)

We Must Never Forget: The Story of the Holocaust. (Library Video)

Web Sites

www.artyzm.com/matejko/poczet/e_poczet.htm

www.poland.pl/info/information_about_poland.htm

www.sarnow.com/poland/TOURISM/warsaw.htm

www.wings.buffalo.edu/info-poland/classroom/children/timelinehist.html

Due to the dynamic nature of the Internet, some web sites stay current longer than others. To find additional web sites, use a reliable search engine with one or more of the following keywords to help you locate information about Poland. Keywords: *Carpathian Mountains, Gdansk, Kraków, Vistula River, Lech Walesa.*

Index